D1165542

Tiny Life on Your Body

By Christine Taylor-Butler

Consultants
Reading Adviser
Nanci Vargus, EdD
Assistant Professor of Literacy
University of Indianapolis
Indianapolis, Indiana

Subject Adviser
Howard A. Shuman, PhD
Department of Microbiology
Columbia University Medical Center
New York, New York

Children's Press®
A Division of Scholastic Inc.
New York   Toronto   London   Auckland   Sydney
Mexico City   New Delhi   Hong Kong
Danbury, Connecticut

Designer: Herman Adler Design
Photo Researcher: Caroline Anderson
The photo on the cover shows the bacteria which causes acne.

Library of Congress Cataloging-in-Publication Data

Taylor-Butler, Christine.
  Tiny life on your body / by Christine Taylor-Butler ; consultant, Nanci R. Vargus.
      p. cm. — (Rookie read-about science)
  Includes index.
  ISBN 0-516-25299-2 (lib. bdg.)   0-516-25480-4 (pbk.)
  1. Body, Human—Microbiology—Juvenile literature. I. Vargus, Nanci Reginelli. II. Title. III. Series.
  QR46.T38 2005
  612—dc22   2005004633

CHILDREN'S PRESS, and ROOKIE READ-ABOUT®,
and associated logos are trademarks and/or registered trademarks
of Scholastic Library Publishing. SCHOLASTIC and associated logos
are trademarks and/or registered trademarks of Scholastic Inc.

1 2 3 4 5 6 7 8 9 10 R 14 13 12 11 10 09 08 07 06 05

Your body has lots of
different parts. Some of
them you can see. What
do you see here?

Other body parts you can't see. They are too small. They are called cells (SELLS). Your body has millions of cells. These cells make up your skin.

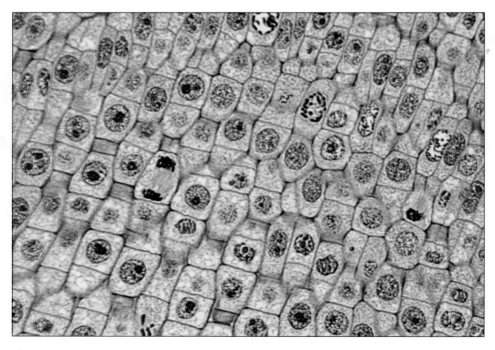

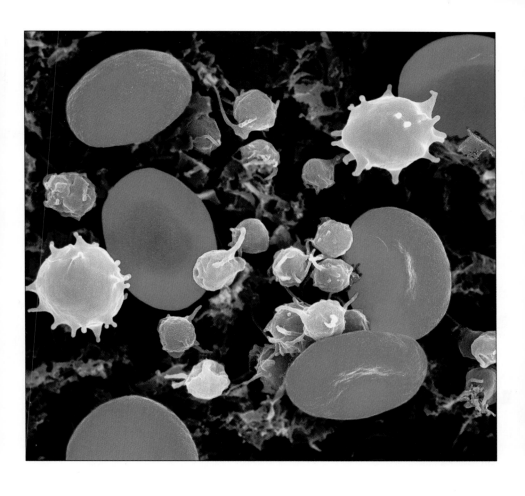

These cells make up
your blood.

6

Your body also has tiny
things that live on it.

Each little circle here is a
tiny life. It has one cell.

Even with one cell,
it can do a lot of things.

One kind of tiny life is
bacteria (bak-TIHR-ee-uh).

Your skin has lots of
bacteria on it. Some
bacteria help you.
They are good bacteria.

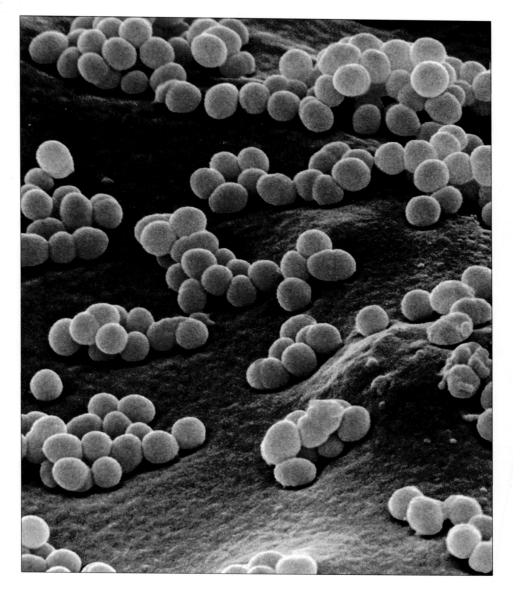

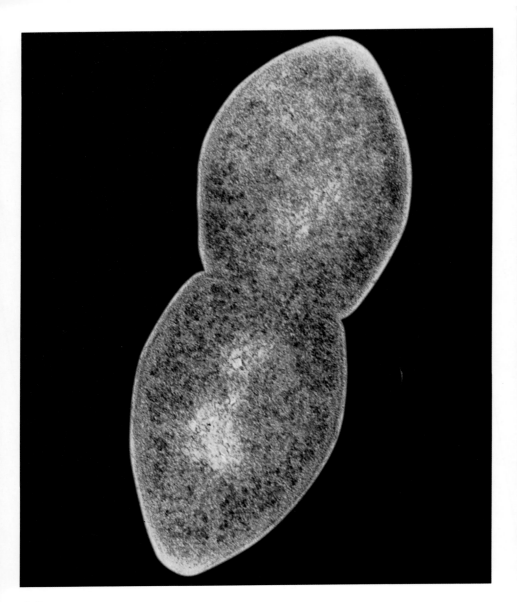

10

Some bacteria can hurt you. Bad bacteria are called germs.

Germs can make you sick. This bacteria makes you sick with pneumonia (noo-MOH-nyuh).

Good bacteria help defend you from bad bacteria.

Good bacteria help your body stay healthy.

13

You can help your body stay healthy, too. You should wash your hands with soap and water.

Some soaps are called antibacterial soaps. These soaps kill bacteria.

Say, "Aah!" Your mouth has bacteria, too. More than 500 different kinds of bacteria may live in your mouth.

17

18

Some bacteria in your mouth are bad bacteria. They cling to your teeth.

This bacteria helps form harmful plaque. You brush your teeth to get rid of the bad bacteria.

Some bacteria in your mouth are good bacteria.

The good bacteria help keep your teeth healthy and prevent cavities.

A virus is another kind of tiny life. Viruses can make you sick.

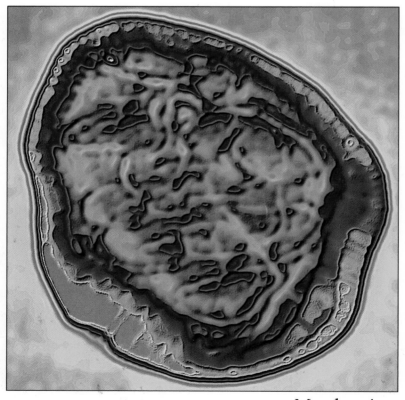

Measles virus

Have you ever had the measles or the flu? They are caused by viruses.

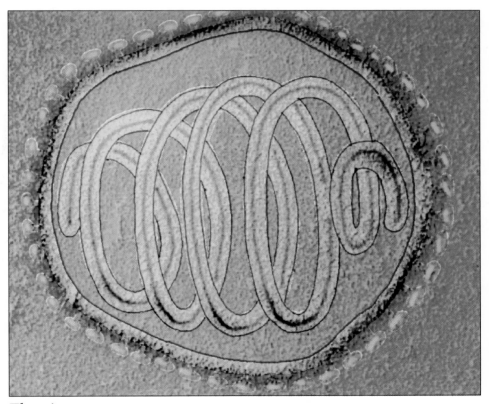

Flu virus

Vaccines (VAK-seens) help your body fight off the harmful viruses.

Vaccines fight off bad bacteria, too. Getting a vaccine may not feel good, but it will help you.

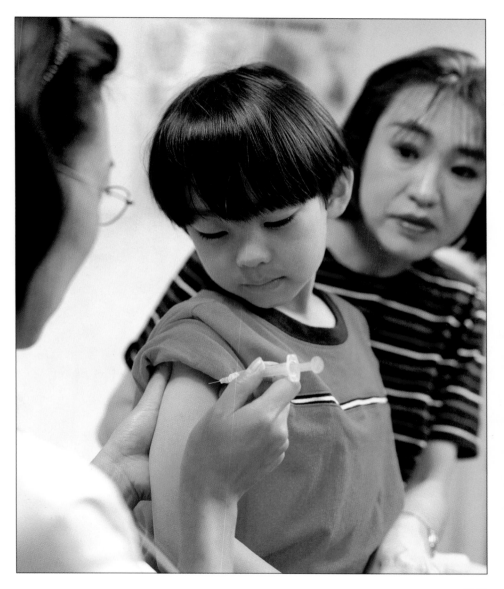

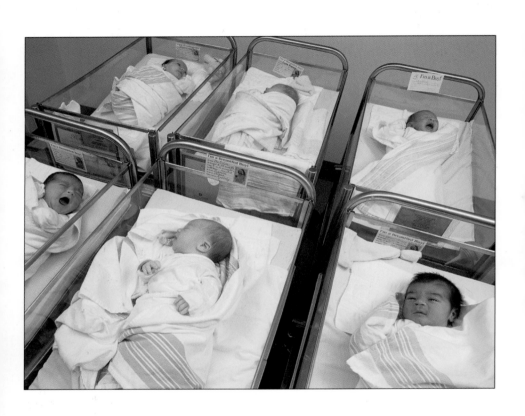

Babies are born without bacteria, good or bad. Within one week, their bodies are full of these tiny life-forms.

Your body needs the tiny life that lives on it. A few may make you sick.

Most kinds of tiny life help keep your body strong and healthy.

Words You Know

antibacterial soap

brush

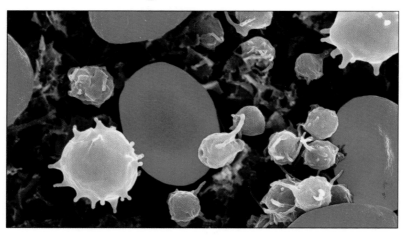
cell

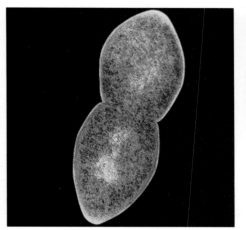

germs

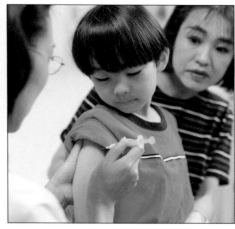

vaccine

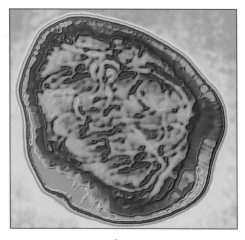

virus

Index

About the Author

Christine Taylor-Butler is the author of nineteen books for children and adults. In addition to her fiction titles, she has written a nonfiction series about the planets. Formerly an engineering manager with Hallmark Cards, Ms. Taylor-Butler holds two degrees from the Massachusetts Institute of Technology. She now lives in Kansas City, Missouri, with her husband, Ken, two daughters, a pride of mischievous black cats, and two tanks of anxious but safely contained fish.

Photo Credits

Photographs © 2005: Corbis Images: 26 (Blaine Harrington III), 3 (Tom & Dee Ann McCarthy), 6 (Charles O'Rear), 13 (Ariel Skelley), 4 (Jim Zuckerman); Digital Vision: 18, 30 top right (Daniel Pangbourne), 29 (Rob Van Petten); Getty Images: 9 (Dr. David M Phillips/Visuals Unlimited), 25, 31 top right (Richard Price/Taxi); Peter Arnold Inc./Manfred Kage: 17; Photo Researchers, NY/Alfred Pasieka: 22, 31 bottom; PhotoEdit/David Young-Wolff: 14, 30 top left; Phototake: 10, 31 top left (Luis M. de la Maza, Ph.D. M.D.), cover (Dennis Kunkel); Stone/Getty Images/Peter Cade: 21; Superstock, Inc.: 23; Visuals Unlimited/Dr. Dennis Kunkel: 5, 30 bottom.